Love *and* Resistance

Theresa J. Wolfwood

Smallberry Press

A CIP catalogue record of this book is available from the
British Library.
ISBN: 978-0-9930315-0-2

Published by Smallberry Press
64 Berberis House, Highfield Road
London TW13 4GP
www.smallberrypress.co.uk

Front cover: lino cut, *justice*, by Oona Padgham.
Back cover: author photograph by Mohamed Sulaiman Labat.

For those I love,
who love life and
believe as I do:
to resist is to exist.

CONTENTS

We are the canaries

We are the canaries
in the mine shaft
of daily fear
of a suffocating end
that we, the world,
even unto the smallest fly,
will die snuffed by poison
emanating from crazed leaders
from profit mad media moguls
from the toxic fumes of lies
that pour
from laboratories
of prevarication
silken words false images
invisible atoms measured into
vessels everywhere
billboards, expert sources,
surveys, sale flyers
policy papers from consultants
restructured
companies, governments
whole countries,
the miasma of conspiracy
so powerful
even the very air we breathe

is threatened.

we are the canaries
smelling the methane
of death and greed
we go ahead
resolute in our rallies,
our meetings, our walks
our words, our deeds become a chorus
bearing witness against prophecy
the deceit of greedy promise.
we sing even in dark places
prisons without light
we sing into open skies
and empty streets
we will sing and sing
until our frail lungs exhale our truth
that will enclose the busy,
the apathetic, the otherwise
occupied with golf courses or cruises
or the magic of malls
and those who have no strength
and lack bread
and those who hear only bullets and bombs
and lack shelter.
we will sing until they all hear us
sing until they lift up and join us
sing until we sing the songs together.

we will be as a host of golden birds
rising from invisible and deep places
we will banish the fear
we will transform the power of desecration
our song will restore the earth
and the sun will rise anew
to celebrate us
on a pure and glistening morning.

Jesus in the parking lot

Just one of a million strip malls
no trees   a slab of wavy pavement
without planters filled with geraniums or lobelia.
A row of no-frills factory outlets
boxes with empty eyes,
boarded windows,
signs for seconds in
outsize jeans,
a gunsmith with double bars,
surveillance cameras,
specials on disposable diapers.

The parking lot   a scatter
of pickups and SUVs,
a few old beaters dreaming
of new chrome and cheap gas,
 bumper stickers
-*America   Love it or Leave it*-
I tried to leave   it was a
mistake   to want to photograph
the store front in the middle
with yard high neon letters:

The Alliance Church of Jesus Christ the King

4

But he waved me down with a baseball cap
so dirty the logo was illegible,
he huddled in an old grey blanket
dripping his scruffy dog
drooped beside him
trying not to look
as his hairy master asked for a ride.
-I've got to get out before the cops come
I asked them for change
enough for a meal for me and Matt here
they said I was too dirty to pray with them,
get a job or get a life
join the army   be a soldier for Jesus in Iraq -

He shivered in the rain
wet toes sticking through ripped canvas.
-Told them I could be Jesus or maybe his cousin -
- *we're calling the cops, dope head* –
- going out the door
one old woman whispered she'd pray for me-
 Matt's too small to be a donkey
but he's my best friend,
so, lady   give us a ride into Bellingham,
Jesus doesn't live here anymore.

An afternoon in March

put away the banners
stack up the placards
the demonstration is over
a few hundred hardy souls
clumped under umbrellas
it always rains in March
weary and dejected
we cleave to friends and home.

we dry out our socks and jeans
drink hot tea to chase the chill
we wonder if anyone cares
what effect we had
do the Saturday shoppers
just think oh not again
those crazy protestors
why don't they get a life?

some fret that media
ignore us and politicians don't
answer letters while bombers
rain down their gifts to the world
somewhere in Asia, Africa,
Latin America, a mother gathers
tiny fragments of almost

weightless legs arms organs.

we drink our tea
and plan the next event
rain or shine.

Oh Palestine

everywhere the pale whispers of olive blossoms
bulldozers gash the innocent earth
puffs of warm bread and snowy yogurt
cruel coils of razor wire obstruct
endless glasses of mint tea
dragon breath of tear gas
dark sweetness of cool dates
sun and sky absorbed in grey gun steel
a chair waits beside generous roses
checkpoints in noon heat emanate cold fear
hear soft laughter savour loving cheeks
insistent ambulances hurdle past

oh Palestine
your broken skin exhales
the steadfast scent of za'atar
oh Palestine.

Hearts

you enter my land break it
with your cruel machines
I watch you bring more soldiers
to guard your destruction
trucks arrive
disgorge relentless blocks of concrete
align them like stones
in a cemetery
you add your garden of razor wire
your trees are
high electric fences
your life is steel and cement
our life greets every dawn
in fractured villages
our trees replanted
as fearful children
still grow beautiful
 your wall
your brutal gift
spans the world
our cause grows
 an olive seed
in the hearts
of good people.

Take up a hammer and a chisel
break down the wall in your heart.

For Mourid Barghouti

In our world of violence
the small, the familiar,
sweet and sad,
acts of love and art,
 are made
even more precious;
my hand strokes the words
of your poems
arranged like empty houses
on the page.

You sit alone
on stony ground,
leaning against the trunk
of a barren olive tree,
you also hold
a page of your poems,
raise your head,
lift your precious cargo,
and read to the hungry bees.

Words float up, lodge
in branches,
become blossoms;
wind drifts their pollen

until it finds my garden
of fir and fern,
it comes to rest on my hand
open on your book of poems.

Mourid Barghouti is a Palestinian poet, living in exile in Egypt.

Fox fur

When you reach for me
the air ripples
as our lovemaking begins
I smell my mother's
exhalations from her camphor chest
squatting at the end of our bed
your arms encircle, heat my bare shoulders
as foxes, rusty red neckpieces
slink from invisible cracks in the chest
their mouths full
each of the other's tail
glassy eyes of taunting sisters watch
they'll tell, I know
as your soft fingers reach my breasts
you murmur *lovely flesh*
I feel the fur caress my ribs
and tickle my knees
I want to watch only you
through today's mirror
your persistent touching
rubbing away the past
of sisters teasing
confirming my foolish self
an awkward child
never taken seriously

my eyes closed
as your arms' hair
warms my body
as no dead animal can
as no other person can
we burrow in each other's' den
mouths possess
and heat flows
present love
closes up the chest
glass eyes shut
past and future vanish
now I inhale only you
and the fresh-picked sweet peas
close by the bed
away from that camphor chest
where fox and siblings
are lost in odourless dust.

The handkerchief

always in the bottom of her purse
a handkerchief
sometimes clean, white, and folded
        or wrinkled with bits of tobacco.

We would take the inter urban into Vancouver
to go to the Carnegie library
named for that rich man –
who had a late life conversion
to philanthropy,
leaving his name on stones hewed
by countless thousands
- their lives cut short
by unrewarded, unheralded, brutish labour.
Mother would take the handkerchief, spit on it,
and rub at my dirt smudged face,
I can smell still the mixture of tobacco, Fleur de Rocaille,
stale leather and paper,
        the earth of her mouth.
She never had colds, but
always had a handkerchief.

As the train pulled out of Victoria station
bound for Southampton,
        a moving clothesline of fluttering handkerchiefs,

she cried for her ageing parents
- she never saw her father again –
her handkerchief
a sodden ball
as sooty London was left behind.
Granny came to live with us – she shed no tear –
believed only that
              heaven or hell
were made here on earth by each of us.
handkerchiefs used to stem blood
from cuts and scratches
                  wore out.

The day came
when I found a forest
of crushed tissues under her bed.

This year my friend, Linda
            died of cancer.
at the library, doing research, I found that
Denise Levertov, a favourite poet,
had just died.
I went outside holding some of her poems,
saw my first hummingbird of the year
clinging bravely
            in the height of a leafless tree
then arcing into magnolia blossoms.
and I read Levertov's words........

"....*into our flesh our*
deaths, crossing the street, plum, quince,
living in the orchard and being
hungry, and plucking
the fruit." *

Driving to the hospital
    to see her for the last time,
I needed no handkerchief,
       sustained by the world
reflected in the eyes of a young
deer standing by Elk Lake
and favourite lines by Dorothy Livesay.

She lay unconscious,
a crumpled stained handkerchief
      on a stretch of dirty snow.

I hoped she was on "...   *a rung on the ladder*
    upwards
    towards a possible
    breathtaking landscape." **

*Denise Levertov in unknown poem
** Dorothy Livesay, 'Bellhouse Bay'

For a friend

too swift her journey
so brief our time
this arrow of brilliance
shaft of energy
radiating light
warming
brief holding
creating love
she pierced the infinite
she marked us
with the assurance
of a calligrapher's brush
her long thin fingers
slipping by
leaving
compassion
ephemeral beauty
grace
insight............
then hurled into
a larger universe
a meteorite shower
of brilliant seconds

transformed our world
an irrevocable gift.........
we remain earthbound
and clutch at her *zeitgeist*.

Just a job

nestled in the pristine mountains
clean air, tall green pines and firs
nice white homes garnished with
lush lawns full double garages
a town of lovingly tended gardens
it's a great place to live.

in the crisp peace of dawn
he gets up to weed runner beans
to deadhead climbing roses
to eat ham and eggs with the family
after he walks the dog   reads the paper
then drops his son at baseball practice.

he drives through guarded gates
to his office deep in a hillside
opens many locked doors
to a secret chapel filled with big screens
and banks of blinking controls
their peaceful hum soothes him.

all day he presses keys   moves images
studies virtual maps of a distant land
his hands command the keyboard

his drones discharge their load
he eliminates six villages before leaving
to take his daughter to a birthday party.

The lace curtain

A gift from her grandmother
now most furnishings were gone
only a few necessities left
the curtain fluttered in
on frail breezes
yellowed and tattered at the hem
but sunlight revealed
intricate patterns
in flowers of unknown origin
profuse in their
intimate intertwining
she could feel her
grandmother's love
she saw the soldiers
through small tears and holes
her glassless windows
gave free entry to the sounds
of guns and shouts of joyful hatred.

The curtain rent by bullet holes
still enough to make her shroud.

A constellation of minute miracles

my tranquillity and isolation abandoned
you led me to the sea for low tide in June
lowest of the year   beyond the slabs
of mottled sandstone populated by a nation
of oysters in meadows of emerald sea plants
they wait for the tide's turn   the oily dark sea
guarded by herons and eagles who consider my presence
a hostile act they depart without haste or fear
as limpets and barnacles gather me into their comity
small pools hold clans of minnows
rocks shelter starfish gleaming porphyry
in this universe of greatness it was your spirit
that drew me to the water's edge I am so feeble
to offer my love in an constellation of minute miracles
a pair of mussel shells the size
of a baby's fingernail lie open at my feet
I thrust my heart in them
throw the sealed cerement at the incoming tide
sea water trickles then rushes behind me
at the safety of the wrack line
below cliffs of shale and hanging ferns

I sit on silvered cedar on the trace
of my imagination and watch Sisyphus
of oceans fling up the sea's bounty where

in a cache of pale shell fragments
as rock unceasingly becomes sand
grows a sturdy plant
with two sun yellow flowers that
face down the incoming tide
stalwart they resist the waves.

For Shaima

At the post office
when I mailed my letter to you
I asked:
is the mail going through to Iraq?
no notice that it is not
was the reply.
I bought the stamp
and sent my greetings.

I am thinking of you and your friends
in the courtyard of
a thousand years old university
where you studied my language
the language of imperialism
the language of greed.

you wore a scarf and giggled
come to the WC and
I will show you my hair
it is very long.

now around me
the voices of death shout
　　we want war
we will kill you to save you

missiles are ready to fly
to destroy your historic city
to kill you
and your widowed mother
and the man you love
and smash your dreams to rubble

in your graduation photo
you and other women wore
special red scarves that day
and you clutched Mickey Mouse.

Mickey Mouse-
a symbol of imperial power
to amuse, to divert, to lie.
Why do you hold it?
while we amuse ourselves
to death   of the soul.
while we starve and bomb
you to death   of hope.
I did not ask, it seems unkind
to cavil at a ridiculous rodent

I sent the most banal of greetings
of wishes for your marriage
even though you have no money
little food
and no job prospects

and my feeble wishes for peace.

you studied George Bernard Shaw
I sent you papers last year about
the irony of an Englishman
who satirised war
as a silly male game
you did well on your thesis.
Shaw was born long
before Disney
now satire is impossible
irony is luxury
the troops are ready
Disneyland is guarded
as carefully as the Pentagon.
symbols are important.

did my letter arrive
before the missiles?
did any plane carry a harmless cargo
to a country tipped
on the chasm of destruction?

will you marry that nice man
in your graduating class before
he takes a uniform
and departs with a gun?
before your dreams become dust?

only if the stamp has more power
than the bomb
only if our words, our voices
our power of peace
can drive the missiles back.

if you ask me, dear Shaima,
I could not answer
but   with only hope
only with a stamp
as the postal clerk
looks sympathetic when
I start to weep before her
will it arrive before you die?

only if
only hope the letter comes
before the bombs,
a letter carried by millions of voices
 a power with no threat
on the desert wind
hear the words:

NO TO WAR.

*In 2001, I met Shaima, an English student, at the Al
Mustensyria University in Baghdad, probably the oldest
university in the world. The USA bombed it in April, 2003.*

Bird child

His skin is tight
pulled without relief
stretched fiercely
over frailest of bones
eroded from within
by gyrating forces
eating his body, even his hair,
reduced to the faintest of fluff.
Through that blued skin
transparent as silk
I see his valiant veins
pulsing a pavan
where the myth of life
fights against
oblivion between
pride and despair.

His fleshless nose
sharp like a hawk's beak
grasps at breath
for his shrivelled
flightless body.
He cries with pale mews
for seconds
in days of silence

his first and only
word...pain...
is the marker of
these suffering, these, his
last days.

I want to wrap
a gift of
seconds, minutes,
hours, days,
weeks, months,
years,
in gossamer bandages tied
with strands
of desert wind.

I will steal them
from CEOs
smug in boardrooms,
grab time from retired generals
playing golf,
suck blood from
retired presidents
by sinking barbed
hooks in their flesh
as they fish on their yachts.
I want to give this child
shrunken

in his crippled shadow
the impossible gift...
the joy
of
free flight.

Your back

I come into our bedroom,
you lie turned away, throw
off the night's cover
warmed by sun's lemon radiance.

your back a mahogany guitar
emerging from its case
insinuates silently the life grain
flows in that glowing light.

my hand brushes the tension of your curve,
below the ribs
your hip holds
a humming echo.

I climb through your branched ribs to hear
life in your heart,
my ear against your singing veins
riffs your rhythmic beat.

There is music in shaped wood,
in curves of bone stretched skin
it takes only an assured hand
to start the song.

Looking for Dayna

Stopped to call Oona
the usual Sunday morning check-in
called from an outside payphone
on the curb beside a Petrocan pump
Smithers on a nice sunny morning
don't remember much
except Gerd putting in a new headlight
dandelions in the pavement cracks
and me stubbing my toe on a crumbling curb
and Oona said –
you ought to visit my friend Dayna
she lives up there somewhere
I can't remember the name of the place
but she'd really like visitors –
so the phone book says she lives in Granisle
but her phone is "no longer in service"
but she's a teacher and school's not out
she's moved in with someone else for sure
no problem small town on Babine BC's largest lake
she'll be easy to find and so surprised to see us
besides we need a hot shower
CBC Sunday morning one of the last a special
on the 50th anniversary of India's independence
an interview with four women writers
who speak English with mango tongues and

nuances of gold threaded silk saris
just when one is describing the menstruation hut
where women of the family were exiled monthly
and the joy of missing chores
a mangy mother moose grazes in the roadside grass
calves hidden in the thicket behind
we go over a hill and lose India
that is we lose the CBC for the time
and know somehow we'd lost it forever as well
the black spruce club at new black clouds
I rush into the town's only cafe and get directions
two blocks up and left to the seniors' home
guess the north is better for the young
they overbuilt the seniors' housing
or maybe the north is an early killer
anyhow the little row house suite is empty
was pounding on the neighbour's door
while the rain pounded me
man in a grey car leaned out
and shouted who you looking for?
she's moved three doors down but she's not home
saw her car on the road a few minutes back
drives off as I climb in the van drenched
let's eat at the cafe where the waitress was so helpful
same man passes again
she's at the school her little red car's there
I knock on doors walls and windows at the school
leave a soggy note in waterproof ink

-Oona's mom at the café- -
the daily special was real homemade mushroom soup
it was good but made with Money's mushrooms
not local wild ones that people pick for good money
they're shipped to Germany and Sweden
they don't eat wild mushrooms there any more
ten years since Chernobyl
posters in Germany said mushrooms never forget
the waitress phones the school for us no reply
so we leave the steamy smoky warmth where
the other waitress sat and smoked silently while we ate
hey there's a ballgame in Topley today
she probably left her car at the school
and went with a bunch of them
another soggy note under the windshield wiper
we left town in a patch of sun down the road
stopped to see the world's longest maternity ward
salmon enhancement program
delivery beds made of evenly sized granite gravel
perfect to cradle fifteen million newborn eggs
and graves for mothers another storm off the lake
Connie Kaldor crooning give me a *canooooe*
all the water of Asia and Africa beside and above us
Rajasthan and Sahara make moose pasture muskeg
ballpark's right on the highway by the school
boy shooting baskets beside Mountie car
moms and kids snacking behind third base
some young jockish women drinking beer

oh no Dayna isn't here
she hurt her knee and stayed home
so Dayna and Mike always make sure to either
be famous or be listed and be happy when it rains
but I hope the sun shines for your wedding
 it did.
last words are Dayna's
 -came out of the school
 was in the photocopy room
saw a red VW van pull out strange
never saw one up here before
maybe parents looking for kids
found the notes and nearly cried
in nine months never had visitors drop in-

*CBC - Canadian Broadcasting Corporation - Canada's
public radio, now suffering from severe funding cuts.
Money's - the BC company that produces most of the
mushrooms we eat here.*

Spring is a foreign country in Palestine

spring is a foreign country in Palestine where
grieving women go mad for the longing
of blossoms
their throats stopped with stones
they scream
in unuttered laments
cries that stick and
 lie heavy   on crumbled walls
some women keen without cease
like sand abrades membranes
screams spew out the raw edges of pain
each agony, each wound,
rends their loss   their children
shriven in xeric desolation

full olive trees
once were saplings nurtured
and loved as family
the fruit of the future
the slow dense twisted mystery
of the bitter plum
of golden oil
the women lean into the rubble
that metastases where once
were homes filled with children's play

and now sons,   even daughters, will not stay

they grieve for villages, houses
grew like sisters beside olive trees
that disappear in maws of steel
that bring hate to life
as real life vanishes
the women watch the ravens
pick through the rubble
global scavengers feast on
misery and destruction

five hundred thousand olive trees
die in agony   limbs fractured
or disappear whole
stolen for victor's profit
victims of war
whose crime is life

and criminals are those who
seek a homeland where
spring should come
with new growth
and the dove returns
only when the branch of peace
regenerates but now women
stare into a bleached and empty sky
doubting life in a landscape where

seasons, land, family
are all foreign countries

in their madness
they build again
kneel in the dust of the past
women dig and plant once more
with work cracked hands
frail seedlings, saplings,
food for the future seasons
and lie with their men
and say: is it madness
to hope   to see
a time when
our seeds live   to multiply
and our homes and orchards
resound with the call of doves?

it is not madness
but   abundance of life
the force that no army
no machine can vanquish
it is abundance of promise fulfilled
they will see, and
so will doubting youth
when spring brings them home
to see the carefree play of children
to see proud men again

take up their hoes
and peace comes
like a downy feather on the breeze
unnoticed until it lights on
a sleeping infant's cheek
when all live in repatriated spring
in green and song scented lands.

Change

From alcoves of dirty snow
mole mounds on a city sidewalk
hands stretch
voices murmur at knee level
any change? spare any change?
It needs a special ear to hear the pleas
 timid, soft and weak
when cars, trucks,
buses blare importance
shoppers shouting, laughing
deafened by sweet siren calls
of glittering goods.

I rush to a high room
above the mere mortal noise of streets
where servers carry
loaded sandwich platters
tubes of aluminium filled
with sweet brown syrup
roll, tinkle, pop behind
the world's most recognised logo.

The aged doyen smoothed her
silk and soft tweed
announces to crowd of deferent acolytes

globalisation is here
there is no alternative
they chorus no possible change
accept, compete, expand
they flap and chirp like grey winter
starlings as they guzzle their global nectar.

Even exhaust fumes smell better
than that rarified opiate stratosphere
back down on concrete earth
now raining on snow
that glistens with a greasy patina.
I walk on through more people
than I will ever know
I meet a young man standing
shabby but alive.

Can you spare some change?
we talk he says - it's bad when it rains
people don't like to stop-
bareheaded with cap in hand
he thanks me as I turn to go
a scarf of words
elusive a dove's flutter
he calls -have a nice weekend-
without thinking I reply
-the same to you-
I feel like a fool.

What is a good weekend for him?
a warm bed? a good meal?
memory of a mother's love?
he is some mother's son
does she still dream for him?
I pass a lighted plastic box
outside a pile of dark cold stone
where God inside is
an upper class Englishman
It glows: Gandhi said
We must be the change we want
to see in the world.   If only.

Summer invasion

The island is under siege
the invasion is in full force
the cadets of the corporate army
stalk with blazing cell phones
tell the world
we are coming
we are coming
as they swarm our little ferries
with their SUVs
loaded with the latest in
expensive bicycles, surf boards
maybe a kayak or boat on top
and their precious mini - cadets
with square eyes
in identi-kit gear crying "I wanna"
apprentice shoppers learn
as they pose
in their uniforms
the latest gear from global
sweatshops
bought in fancy stores
the same stuff everywhere
covered with labels
from hat to marching shoes
medals of consumption

like colour coordinated caterpillars
they exhibit the latest fashion
only security of conformity
can give them comfort
superiority
as they mock
the shabby locals
in their last year's
recycled gear or
even tie-dyed shirts
 such a time warp
 this rustic place
of stone and sea
of big trees and handmade homes
 is better than a video
and armed with cash cards
and the ammunition of easy wealth
they can buy anything
artsy or quaint
bar codes are their service stripes as
happy trophy hunters go back to the city
plan their next excursion
find an even more pristine place
to overrun with even more bucolic
locals with long shaggy hair
to patronise and smile down at
as they formation
fly in unconscious squadrons

seeking novelty
afraid of continuity
context and history because
if they ever stop shopping
they might have to connect the dots.

Helliwell Park

The tallest firs sway
topped by finials
lethal eyed eagles
they flute love calls
to life mates and
wait for herring
to silver the cold steel sea
skittish cormorants
break across
the surface water
waves carry broken
bassoons of braying sea lions.

When under bowed arbutus
elusive and elegant as
a wind tossed leaf
happiness encircles us
in radiant dance
it gentles down
around our shoulders
the knowingness of it
permeates us
seeps our bones into
the sandstone
we transcend time

and timelessness
we gather the grace.

I hold the feeling
in close embrace
clasped ready for
dark days coming
when I cloak
myself in memories
dream back into this time
and cling to the benison
of a day
when imbued
with love's power
we did not see
the future beyond the cliffs.

Your dream

you roared like a wounded bull
frightening the weak dawn
I awoke rigid and alert
and tipped like a canoe
spilling love and fear
as I shook you awake
all the contingency plans
swirled in my head nitroglycerin
911   doctor's phone number
what's wrong? where is the pain?
your eyes opened
puzzled you smiled *I'm fine*
I had a dream, I guess
there was a man all in black
standing still
at the foot of the bed
you smiled again and
went back to sleep
I rolled over
and the earth sighed
languid beneath me
Schubert's eighth echoed
I thought every life
is an unfinished work,
but- no not yet please-

when I tried to sleep
the black clothed man reappears
to me silent without music
I wondered when will he return to stay?

the sun's first light played
on your still quilted back.

Dalit

I wondered
if I touch the skin
gentle
on your perfect cheek
that the pain
born of history
would explode
from your bones.

When our hands
clasped
I felt the hard geography
of your resistance.

In the open sky
of your radiant face
I saw dance
I heard song
you and your sisters
together resolute
on the path towards
freedom's golden horizon.

Dalit: we used to call them Untouchables.

To a gift box of chocolates

wrapped in pictures of Swiss snowy mountains,
quaint castles, pristine lake scenes
they shoulder so snugly against each other in sealed
squares where the alps shelter the smooth brown
chocolate designed to melt on the receiving
tongue   wafers of warm bliss give
moments of ecstatic oblivion to all who taste
but this pleasure has no history
in postcard pictures that hide small
children who hugged their mothers
clung to their brown warmth but were cleaved away
and sold somewhere else in Africa where days are
filled with a sun that can melt chocolate and memory
all day these waifs hack small fruits that
hug their mother tree and her limbs
golden pods that enclose the precious cocoa
in the heat drenched night in a crowded hut
their fear and sadness overcome in the thick blackness
they sleep exhausted shoulder to shoulder
oblivious of rats and factories where rivers
of smooth dark chocolate flow into neat forms
and harden for our greed and delight
these captured children sold as slaves
for our succulent desires shrivel and starve
sicken, beaten and bruised they fall on hostile foreign

ground an end to pain and hunger would be
a benisonas there can be no possibility of relief
never will they savour that worshipped wafer
on their sere tongues, never will see castles
on glacier green lakes snug beside snowy mountains.

Claudia and her sisters, El Mozote

Behind these women stands a memorial a tribute
a list of names all those who died this week
twenty five years ago in El Mozote
 left lifeless by brutal murderers

today girls confirm life in daily work a baby cries
answered soon in the security of the breast
an act of faith an act of endurance Phoenix-like families
rose from the ashes and bodies of the massacre

like fabled birds people recreated birth
life hesitantly began anew now laughter
mingles with bird song the sound of water
and chatter of children Claudia waits watchfully

for her communion dress a white dove
at rest in a red basin waits for the signal
to fly above the ruins to meet life under
a sun circled by a multitude of guardian spirits.

Nuts and stones

*For Hilary Newitt Brown 1909-2007 and Virginia Woolf
1882-1941*

fir and cedar forests guard the orchard,
apples are over now, nuts fall in mossy grass
shaken by slender strands of a once fierce
wind exhausted from the resistance
of grey stone slabs shaping the bay below
where the rhythm of waves
rises and falls in constant cataracts.

I set out to the bay to watch the storm
my pockets filled with hazelnuts
my hands roll them and caress their
intimate brownness together with comradely warmth
I veer away from the grey breaking waves where
stones, small and smooth, lie under my feet in millions
their glacial history would chill my fingers
their weight would strain the fabric of my coat.

Virginia must have had cold hands already
when she set out on her final walk
alone towards the River Ouse
she had a literary bond a meeting
of minds in print with my friend Hilary

a nurturer of trees, fruit, peace poppies and people
who died after the fullest of lives at ninety-eight.

I wonder if Virginia might have found peace
from her torments on this small island
-a peaceful place so close to paradise-
and walked these shores with stalking herons,
streaming pipers and a companion
like Hilary, soothed by warm nuts
in deep pockets as they talked about their work
and ideas for social change.

would she have chosen life
and returned to the orchard for more
refusing as I do now the unforgiving waters
to leave them to fulfil their Sisyphus task
dragging and shifting centuries of stone.

know that the relentless power of
water and wind can kill or create.

*Hilary wrote "Women must Choose" in 1937 (Gollancz,
UK) which Virginia Woolf quotes in "Three Guineas"
(Hogarth Press, 1938). Both books have been described as
feminist and anti-fascist.*

Hilary and her husband immigrated to Hornby Island, BC,

Canada in 1937 fearing a fascist victory in Europe. They never left. Hilary was an environmental, peace, and community activist there for 70 years, living on the beautiful property which became, as a result of her initiative and generosity, the Heron Rocks Friendship Centre.

Fences

Cows know better than to try,
pacific, brown and white
they graze slowly, patiently
every blade of green grass
chewed and chewed again
until it becomes white milk,
with no curiosity of such a miracle,
about the other side of the fence,
thin and frail, it could not hold in a calf,
but the news has travelled by swishing tails
and startled lowing calls of pain
or birds pecking seeds from warm pies
pass the warning -
to push, to touch, to challenge, to defy
that strange pulsating power hurts too much
until it doesn't matter
soon if the fence is powered or not.
they never try again or bother
to care about the grass
on the other side of the fence
or the winding serpents of concrete, asphalt
and speeding, thundering traffic racing
somewhere with no return.
Life is not all that bad
inside the fence.

Other powered fences shimmer,
sinuously ribbon the equator,
national boundaries,
wind through communities, around
our homes, our dreams, our longing for love,
fences that seem to be solid walls
of sightless eyes facing inward
everywhere, moving images, layered sounds
pulsate a different, more lethal power.

each of us, now alone
we sit on deracinated clumps
our backs to the shadows on the
walls of the cave without thought
of other vistas, our eyes
wired to a greater eye as we chew
squeezed dead cow trapped
between slabs of dead wheat,
our cud of circuses and cake,
 unnoticed small miracles die
unborn at our feet, we drift apart
in separation until all we know,
feel, understand seeps out through
our sated brains, our numbed senses,
slave to distant Tantalus,
our vision and lost visions suspended
in light blindness, stars are obliterated,
our reality fused to transmissions

of controls unknown,
we fear the wisdom of darkness,
we believe and are happy
that there is nothing better outside
our landscape of pulsating glitter
and that life is really
not all that bad inside the fence.

Past love

Round hips hang beside furred galls
yet the scent of spring roses
drifts ghostly sweet
in the cool evening darkness
as I brush past,
my memory recalls
the mixture of soap, sweat,
sawn cedar
that his skin exuded
after love making,
the prickly reluctance of
his attentions.

A modern tale
trite in its commonness
of escape from commitment
pleasure so deep
that the waving trees were
out of sight
until I shifted and curved
and sighted with distance vision
his approach was really
a mirrored sheen of retreat.

He was the Witty's Lagoon

of my solace.
for years I rubbed my bruises,
revisited the winter trickle
of the falls,
then, in spring, the torrent.
I loved the deceptive calm
in the ever shifting pool,
the apple orchards,
tangled fir and arbutus,
the sound of water lapping
worn unresisting pebbles
until I saw the world without him,
in its own diverse moods.
now I love that lagoon
without aetiology
 for itself alone, for being.

My moment of cure
 was a late coming,
on a sunny fall day
 in an outdoor market.
full of harvest apples,
I recognised
with a tingle in my fingers
his back long, sinuous
slightly bowed by great height.
he heard me laugh
at a friend's remark,

turned to look
and slipped away past ripe pumpkins.
the young adoring lover, clinging
as she gazed up,
did not see his inattentive smile
transformed to a smirk.

Once I had a son

once I had a son
with hair like gold
bleached in Africa became
a mirror of the sun
so unusual in its fairness and
so straight like straw in fall's thatches
even in the midst of protests when
tear gas streamed from hurled canisters
students bent to touch his head
to stroke the lucky gold
to hear him laugh
to touch and talk to the foreign child.

later in summer solstice in Norway
when sunsets slipped slowly over
a stretching horizon
the same sun shone strong for most of
the northern night on a beach
my son ran to the sea
played with others whose colours
matched his fairness
when I looked
I could not see him in the strands

so many golden boys together
I searched
lost him for hours
soon I lost him forever.

Old and young

she was suddenly old a strong healthy woman
peasant stock used to work and hardship
awareness was difficult to realise
her mortality her fragility she filled with
more fear with each new ailment became bad tempered
and bitter her husband younger and healthier
became the housekeeper then her nurse
she could no longer travel to meetings, classes,
conferences to speak her ideas to organise action
a writer of many books she decided to write her memoir
whenever she had strength to go to her desk
a final act of sadness and defiance
lying in bed she was angered by the crying, shouting
stamping of a small boy in the apartment
above through walls and floor–ceiling
she felt his violence penetrate her mind and body
she felt violent herself and hated the child
one day she arose and opened her door
called the boy down the stairs to her kitchen
together they started to create a story
every day he came they talked wrote
drew pictures made small things
her strength and good nature returned
the boy and the old woman began to love
to understand each other she continued her memoir

the boy ended his noise and violence at home
one day the story came to a happy ending
she needed this last story to end her memoir
she was happy and content with her final creation
the boy was happy and content
with his first of many stories.

Maggie's leaving

First her foundation, rouge, powder, lipstick
then her mascara many layers
one on top of the other like fat spiders' legs
yesterday's perm kept her curls stiff and tidy
dressed and ready to face the world
bedding folded by the door
carved leather vanity case a souvenir
of their bus trip to the casinos in Vegas
trailer spotless no trace she had ever lived there
her old Toyota rusty but still reliable
loaded with dish set, linens, garment bags
her china horse ornaments wrapped in doilies.

Buddy the budgie was chirping for attention
she covered the cage to silence him
house plants in the trunk already
she gave away the ones that couldn't fit in
and leftover groceries to Nellie next door
now just before eight and time to go
she'd have a last breakfast at the Princeton bakery
say good bye to Gladys the morning shift cook.

Buddy and vanity case wedged in the front seat
then one last check   she found not
a single speck of soap or tissue left behind

she did not look into the living room where
Bert's old chair still held the shape of his body
the dent of his head in the brown velour cushion
she would not cry   knew her mascara would run
closed the door gently and whispered good bye
softly so Bert's spirit would not stir.

right on 8 am pulled out of the trailer park
turned towards town and the highway
head high   curls in place   she did not look back
did not see or hear Bert's daughter rev into
the driveway gravel spraying
from the bucking wheels of her big red 4x4.

in the sweet morning sun Maggie had
Buddy and Connie Kaldor
to sing her down the Tulameen valley
heading out for the last time.

South of Batoche

still able to climb through barbed wire fences
we are two women old in friendship and age
together we roam the prairie
we photograph the history of abandonment
farm houses vacant eyed, rusting tractors,
windmills without sails creak slowly
over collapsed chicken coops
under an endless flat sky
we crawl over tipped feed troughs, navigate in coarse grass
send indignant sparrows to their perch
on unwired power poles
at last we reach the Cadillac we sighted from the road
it was young when we were young when
chrome and oil were everlasting
 the open road our right
its seats once by day the resting place
of complacent owners
at night the tryst of writhing lovers
now home to multitudes of mice families
the glove compartment shelters rabbits
the grill still resplendent sweeps its path upward
to forgotten dreams hidden in empty light sockets
a caragana now grows through the motor
green and newly leafed
 it waves in the perpetual prairie wind

this old Cadillac has found the perfect final resting place
open to sun and snow, a refuge for new life beautifully
alone without the indignity of scrap dealers and vandals

we trek about this almost holy place
and decide to will our ashes to be
buried with the roots of
the caragana behind the gleaming grill
and when we get bored with subterranean life
of mingling with molecules of other past lives
after we meet a few Dumonts* that blew down
 from the riverbanks up north and we sense
 the native child who choked to death on diphtheria
 the unnamed settlers who broke this heavy soil
 and died old and frail of influenza
we'll drift out and go for a cruise
the steering wheel's gone you can steer
by the sun hanging loose above the wide prairie

I'll climb the caragana and be lookout for
our children who won't approve of our restless
spirits roaming the prairie
we'll do it anyhow time to defy them
the ultimate privilege of the safely died and gone.

* Gabriel & Madelein Dumont lived in Batoche, a village and meadows on the banks of the North Saskatchewan River, where a museum commemorates those who fought in the Riel Rebellion (of the Metis people) against the government of Canada; Dumont was Riel's partner in the rebellion. Riel was hanged, but Dumont was not & he died later in Batoche in his old age. Batoche is now a National Historic Site near Saskatoon.

Signals

cattle clamber together in confusion
leave their calm grazing
press flank to flank under a tree
and paw the dust with uneasy hooves

the dog's insistent bark rouses the sleeping
shepherd who has no choice but
to follow the sheep dog-driven to
a shady overhanging cliff

snakes who love the sun on hot stones
slither into dark cracks followed by a slink
of cat who forgets her taste for snake
leaves her perch heeding their haste

flowers not understanding the mystery
close blossoms tight in fearful
anticipation of an untimely night under
the trembling leaves of a massive tree

in river pools the fish dive deep
lie still on gravel beds where no food
can be found but on the surface
insects swirl in sudden confusion

swallows, bee-eaters and other
perpetually feeding birds leave
the clouds of insects and
seek their nests but do not sleep

nearby are people, men gossip
women prepare meals and sooth
babies whose cries may be signals
the adults take no heed and carry on.

Stadia   1973 – 1995

After the film*, driving home
in this calm land
we pass the stadium,
    white lit like a heated oven.

Field hockey players swirl
    in the dance of sport
their cries rise and fall
    like dust motes in joined light circles.

We discuss that we admired
Pablo Neruda, in the film just seen,
    serene as the Andes, prophecy
abandoned,   his past composed in metaphors.

He was ill and dying...when it happened
    in the stadium of Santiago a crucible
of cries rising and rising
against the perpetual mountains.

Victor Jara singing, handless,
    sinews streaming blood
replace guitar strings,
until the white heat of bullets explodes his heart.

Those that live go hungry and silenced.
Neruda said...Poetry is like bread...
poetry is bread and millions kill
and die in agony for the lack of a crust.

* *Il Postino* is an Italian film about the friendship of
an Italian postman and Pablo Neruda.

The arpilleristas

It is the love that sustains their every stitch. Broken and
shattered by loss and murder, daily poverty to fuel
massive wealth weighted by warehouse of weapons
and phalanxes of brutalized young men. Women search
for a tomato, a beef bone, a scrap of fish. They scrub
floors on bony knees. Always under aprons an image
of a disappeared beloved, against still beating waiting
hearts. Arpilleristas sew with scraps of clothing not
worn now, only scented memories of happier times.

They open their veins to find thread to sew reality. Strip
sinews to letter a banner ¿Donde Estan?
In frozen moments of rest their silent needles
pierce the sacking, re-create lost families,
show the world their life of soup kitchens, communal
bread ovens, stolen electricity, they create with anger and
sadness rallies to show their resistance, they harvest their
dreams of peace with fruit trees bearing in abundance
for all who share the gathering, in little happy figures
fastened against unending sunrises over the Andes
they stitch that courage is always possible.

Their hope renews every day in the chilled morning
sunrise. Love never sets in the evening ocean. Life
with the disappeared continues. Their faith
embroiders perpetual remembrance on vivid arpilleras.

(E) mail order bride

she slept in a smooth narrow furrow
a long white taproot seeking nurture
he twisted and
swirled in a clumped nest
his feet, hands, elbows, ears flopped
like ravenous eagle young.
when she   without noise or disturbance
slipped her place
 padded into the toilet
he heard her waters rushing from
cave to stream hurrying to the sea.
she returned   silently
he knew her gown was wrapped
around her ankles like a pale datura blossom
he pulled the quilt away and hunkered over her
rolled her roughly   tore the gown her thighs
did not hear the rip of silk   the gasps
puffed into the soft pillow.
 her buttocks glowed
two perfect still frightened rabbits
when he thrust into them
braying above her faint cries
faster louder as the hounds tearing at
 the prey until with one final howl
he fell roiling on her shadowed back

half biting   half sucking
her small right shoulder bone.
he crawled off   rubbed his foetid skin
into the snow of cool mounded bedding.

she willed herself deeper
into the dark earth below.

Phoenix of Babylon

honeyed by the lowering sun
walls of   Babylon cluster
around history of one stone lion
too heavy for looters
sturdy leaves and stalks
push through rubble
 that once enclosed
a queen's lush garden.

the archaeologist walks in
ancient bitumen bricked tracks
and speaks as though
King Nebuchanezzar II
is a recently departed dear friend
we try to see an exquisite glow
from a golden chariot
burnish these honeyed walls.

behind him from a crevice in
shaded crenulations
a kingfisher soars
steals the sun to polish
his azurite, turquoise,
 jasper feathers,
spreads a skein of brilliant hues

as he dives to the palm sheltered river.

around our heads in shimmering halos
colours of old Babylon flash
in dust motes of countless millions
from the lives of residents
millennia past reincarnate in today's soil
the partly rebuilt ancient halls
roofless to the sky and its creatures
hold lost dreams.

Cries echo, echo, echo,
from every patted, stamped brick,
the sweating chants of celebration
of an awesome sun god
trickster kingfisher flashes
by fools us into optimism
the prophet from the Tigris
promises a return of jewelled splendour.

the archaeologist says goodbye
-I will remember you,
you knew the bird-
we walk away from history

confront the reality

the future of barbarism
fall into lengthening silent
 shadows of a fractured present.

Where were you?

my friend said it
-where were you
when we went to war
against Iraq?

he said- I was in Ottawa
my feet freezing at 20 below
watching limousine after limousine
sweeping black through
the snow scape to deliver the MPs
to deliver the vote-
yes, we want war.

in Victoria pansies and primulas
bloomed in the planter
by the harbour
all nice for American tourists,
I climbed up on its brick edge
and said to the sombre crowd...
-this is the saddest of days,
the peace movement has failed,
we see the first post-Cold War
war- power unwrapped
steel and force without fear of reprisal.

ten years later
at two o'clock in the morning
squeezed in a crowd
with drums pounding
chants in Arabic
in English-
down, down, with the USA-
students cheer
 as flared with gasoline
 stars and stripes burn
to a sliver of ash.

Speeches condemn the sanctions
outside the Palm Beach Hotel,
yes that is its name
for this country is
the home of palms
dates the food of gods
 and wheat for
bread for the world.

I meet and photo a man with his family
one would have been a baby
ten years ago.
did he rush his nursing wife
to a bomb shelter as the bombs whined
in the night air?
and then, too close, they saw

smashed, burned, exploded,
a school, a bridge, a shop or
a neighbour's home

They were there ten years ago
as I spoke in the winter's gloom
across the world.
Why would I want to kill
this family, this little girl
with round coals of eyes
under Freda Kahlo's eyebrows?

Ten years later, I am here
in the crowds of Baghdad,
I know where I am, but
I still don't know why
we kill and kill and kill.
Maybe one day
a black limousine
will arrive with the man
with the answer.

Until then I wonder...
is she the child who died
one month later while
I looked again at pansies
 and primulas in Victoria?
I will never know and

I still don't know why.

Where were you?
Where are you now?

Oh, the holly and the ivy

On this morning when radiant sky melds with
shimmering sea
clad in heavy clothes, sturdy gloves,
 we take axes, clippers, shovels
hurry to grasp a few hours of brief respite
from cloud and damp
through bushes and contorted oaks
we trudge to uproot the rampant foreigners
that dare to dwell in our pristine park
for **the holly and the ivy, now are both well grown**
cherished by homesick English colonists
this invasive English culture chokes fragile natives
on Hornby Island yes we know and see well.

 in the rising of the sun and the running of the deer
the holly bears a berry as red as any blood
the holly bears a prickle as sharp as any thorn
We chop, we cut, we destroy
 but save some boughs for home to remind us
we too came with the bird-scattered berries
 and tendrils of cloying ivy thriving on earth, fences walls
creeping into abandoned homesteads to shine in shade
our hands gripped by pain, our faces scratched
we leave exhausted, laden with boughs and vines
and the certainty that our task is as hopeless

as our return to some distant land
that holly's ancient power cannot ward off modern evil
the holly and the ivy, now are both well grown
rooted we are together in this brief borrowed paradise.

Bold lines from traditional English carol.

The passing parade

They march from the fortress
with a single mind
stream down their track
in a wild meadow of grass
a trough of bare earth where
nothing dares to thrive
the queen commands
they obey in frightening precision
without pause or doubt
from their tower of dead fir needles
well-guarded secret within
they seek for substance to carry back
no concern for bulldozers, poison
interference of any outside force
ants know only the daily imperative.

Nicaragua, 1986

the path through the shaded forest
opens to sunlight ends at the wide river
silver ripples net over dark stones
flowing down from green mountains
she steps from the shade stands
on the water's edge in her bright dress
her hair full, dark and wavy glistens
she found a stub of lipstick gloriously scarlet
slicked it on her full lips by the shard of a broken mirror
before she left her village in lush in coffee fields
for the river with her infant son cradled to her breast
she slips off her shoes and lifts them
crosses them on her head of curls
bare legged with skirt held up
she fords the river with confidence
steps on the path her land journey resumed
she slips into her sling back pumps
straightens her skirt arrives at the clinic
where dozens of other mothers in their finery
present babies proudly   chatter and laugh
above the short cries as doctors do their work
one fear allayed for parents seeking
todos los dias maiz y paz

mothers and infants return to families

to villages under a still hot sun
light fires grind corn for tortillas
sooth children, wash them
and caress them to sleep

night slinks down dense mountain slopes
 concealing boys pretending manhood
preening in uniforms
as they wait for signals
clean their guns exchange obscenities
to hide memory and fear mostly memory
caress the smooth grey metal
count bullets below a unstarred infinity
even the moon has disappeared in fists of cloud
those boys silently file on invisible trails
they cradle guns to their breasts
sweating hands on cold steel
curse their blindness stumble into
one another try not to think of their mothers
they hone in on sleeping villages
remember only their orders to shoot and kill
babies lie in peace beside their mothers.

birds at dawn awake over night's carnage
yet chorus unceasingly for hope.

Seeing in the dark

clouds of sand were horizon and sky
the pitiless sun penetrated
seeking life to suck dry
by day the travellers stitched themselves
into crevasses and caves
relief from heat and hurtling silica
crystals that cut the skin
bombard the eyes
yet another hostile force threatened more
this slender band of women children
old and feeble

in daylight planes hunted their journey
phosphorus bombs and napalm
were deadly rain on the desert canvas
at night when wind and sun where gone
when planes returned to base
pilots to eat drink their fill
the group shared their precious little
buried a baby too weak to suckle
and stumbled onward
the stars their atlas and compass
reading the sky like pages of a book
from Orion's belt to the Milky Way
they followed east until dawn

once going on in morning light
seeking refuge too late
a single bomber killed a few old men
the navigator a grandmother
 blinded by phosphorus lived in pain
the broken band folded into
a narrow cliff until night came again
the blind grandmother still saw the stars
as younger women gave the sky to her
they continued diminished determined
burying a few more children
the nights so cold but clear
safe with ancient light and comfort

one night the grandmother stopped
said the faraway is now nearby
they crept along in weary silence
children had no strength to cry
they smelled smoke
heard familiar voices
soon they were lifted gently
like bags of bird bones
given tea food water blankets and peace
journey safely over but memory
slowly released fear and longing

the blinded navigator slept
the stars faded in her internal sight

she saw instead light
the silver glint of ocean waves
palms rustling in oases
she hears water on rock
laughter and camel bells.

Hornby winter

our deer are small, dainty
barely bigger than a sheep
slender seemingly frail yet
capable of great standing jumps
over towering garden fences
persistent in their love of lettuce

when the snow falls and falls
creates an alien landscape
no living earth visible in
the revenge of the rain god
the deer with legs like
hinged knitting needles flounder
they cannot reach their secure
medium of weightless air

a pair of yearlings, stumble
exhausted to your woodshed
stable ground to stand again
quiver in fear and weakness
but content to chew the bark of
fresh alder firewood in safety
gnaw the heat of our winter's desire
return it to the dormant earth.

Birds and the beast

the Hereford steer boldly
defends his meadow
commands the summer grass
holds the shade under trees where
it loiters after a long lunch
a cloud of grey bushtits
swirl around disturb his peace
but they merit only
a desultory tail swish
they skitter away into the maples.

winter comes the now empty
field floods until muddy ice
conceals the ground
the steer is nowhere to be seen
the bushtits at my bird feeder
swoop nervous like giant moths
to perch and cluster upside up
upside down and sideways as
they relish their winter treat
- fresh suet.

The news from Gaza

In the stained and soiled operating theatre
"Take some kittens, some tender little
moggies in a box," said Jamal, a surgeon
at Al Shifa, Gaza's main hospital.

The nurse holds a blood-stained cardboard box
"Seal up the box, then jump on it with all your
 weight and might, until you feel their little bones
 crunching, until you hear the last muffled little mew."

"Try to imagine what would happen
if we do this, and the images were circulated.
Hear the righteous outrage of public opinion,
 the complaints of the animal rights organisations..."

He continues, looking at the box, "Israel trapped
hundreds of civilians inside a school
as if in a box, including many children,
crushed them with all the might of its bombs."

"The world barely reacted... we would have
been better off to be cats rather than Palestinians;
we would be more protected." All eyes are
on the bruised box. He opens the box.

Inside are amputated limbs, legs and arms,
some from the knee down, others with
the entire femur attached, amputated
from the injured of Al Fakhura school in Jabalia.

Based on a news report

We are still here

Last night we went to the seashore
my father carried my little brother
he cries a lot and hardly moves.
mother held the baby
my older brother and I carried blankets
they aren't heavy, we only have a few
nights in Gaza are cold
we wear all our clothes and snuggle together
our house has no walls or roof
so we are accustomed now to lie
under the dark sky
when we are hungry mother says
count stars and we do until we sleep
we reached the beach slowly
the stones hurt my feet because
my shoes have stone-size holes
I don't cry because mother says
I am eight now a big girl
little brother cries for all of us
father hardly ever talks
he walks all night holding my sick brother
this night we wanted to stay awake
under our blankets we waited
lying on a patch of pebbles and sand
the sea so quiet we could hear

the murmurs of hundreds of people.
we were told ships were coming with medicine
and cement to rebuild our house
we try every day to pile up broken blocks
even I can carry small bits
but they don't stay together very well
we waited happy to know help was coming
father has a little job in the day
he used to be a teacher but the school
has gone he sells cigarettes beside the road
I did sleep until my mother shook me
the stars had left the sky
-we go home now she said
the ships won't come they were captured-
we bought a fish from a fisherman
to cook at home for breakfast.
as the sun came up I stumbled along.
father said nothing but I want to say
-please tell your friends
 we are still here in Gaza.

Winter garden

It looks dead or at least dormant
bare twigs at the mercy
of every storm
decaying leaves in hummock over
next year's tulips
I see the scuffle of solemn hooded juncos
optimistic chickadees flutter around
finches muscle in for food
the odd nuthatch hurtles through
a miniature stealth bomber swooping for seeds
a lone towhee is the brightest flash
nervously hiding its Joseph's coat in the bay bush
seeking not just food but sanctuary
last year there was a pair
I found the remains of one left
by a grey feral cat
towhees mate for life.

Winter poem

Greet the darkness with joy
time to rest without
scrutiny of those who judge or mistrust
Darkness is a place of intimacy
our skins merging in double warmth
fingers reaching for fingers clasp in
the blessed lull before the blasts of
too much light that can confuse

Let us enfold ourselves in the tapestry of love
darkness is all the permission we need.

The tapestry of Kabawil

Francisca pulls her threads
leans back on her belt and warp
her loom taut from
the old pine tree to her waist
beside the clavel bush
bleeding its teardrop blossoms
she weaves a brilliant bird
soon reaches the part
where she finishes its upright body
glowing with jewelled feathers
to form two-headed bird Kabawil
in Qucihe this bird of wisdom
roosts above all life
with one pair of eyes
she sees the past in centuries
with her other pair she views
the vastness of the future
the present slips briefly into
the angle where her two heads meet
light and dark good and evil
humans and nature
she sees all simultaneously
a whole tapestry of woven colours
earth sky blood life light
when Kukulcan god of wind

invades the lush clavel
her vision is seared
by the pain of knowledge
tears drops from clavel blooms
fall like a rain of blood
the past cries out in pain
Kabawil cannot teach the future
or heal soil stained by weeping flowers
the present always bleeds
unborn infant and futile hope
Kabawil knows in sadness sees
with lidless eyes past is prophecy
Francisca weaves until
the two heads are looking at her
eyes bright full of questions
she cannot fathom or answer

she sees feet running by under her gate
hears shouts and music in Parque Central
she slips free of threads
folds her tapestry
Kabawil watches
high in her perch as
Francisca runs out to join the future.

Tara's birches

this landscape of birches
mirrored into infinity
reflecting each other
in luminous white bark
endless deep and deeper
I penetrate the captured light
where each birch makes
curls of bark, ever renewed
in season of sweet green promise
dripping catkins until
tired golden leaves crumple
bare branches wait for snow cover

I am dead woman walking
into becoming transformation
reluctant metamorphism
when the anticipated snow
pillows settle over me until
spring comes to open the earth
tentatively leaves unfurl
the heat of a dying sun captured
on the yellow earth

another birch tree is born
infinity expands
I join the whispered conversation
of rustling curls of bark.

Nightfall in the Zocalo

They come marching in lines as sharp
as the crease in their pants soldiers
appear from every corner of the square
 immense in stone and cement
known to be the largest square in all the Americas
sun falling as vendors pack up their wares
from pan pipes to potato chips
from blankets to books
from sweet grass smudges to pop CDs
waiting people form their own precise
square around the flag pole

The flag moves gently
 immense itself maybe
the largest in all the Americas
soldiers salute and file in formation
guns at ready shoes polished
buckles gleam in the sun
now disappearing leaving only shadows
all eyes are on the flag
big enough to roof a dozen peasant homes
slowly it lowers to waiting
arms held out to grasp it
never to be defiled by touching earth
the band calls out the national anthem

the rolled-up flag now marched in
precision movement to waiting trucks
by soldiers who never give even a
 glance to the silent watchers
passive still in their own lines
the country's grandest symbol
must be protected from darkness
as the trucks disappear
people let out a collective sigh
wander off slowly in every direction
chickens seeking food to scratch
just before light leaves
 a hundred white paper doves
lift above the milling people
swooping up and down
in the wind from the square's
severe palaces of religion
 commerce and rulers
the doves fly their own song
 know their own direction
for safety they seek earth's dark places.

City night

strange silence in big city
spring leaves absorb sound
sleepless in a strange bed
I see a dull electric haze
through the window
then sounds startle me
rhythmic repetition of engines
steel on steel on steel

a train loaded with freight cars
mounting speed heading west
 recedes to silence
rails opening to forest and prairie
endless skies
for years the unemployed hobos
jumped freights looking for work
adventure a problem later
 solved by war
the ultimate employer

thoughts of my friend Star with
companions banjos guitars
and dogs riding the rails last fall
not knowing what future
meets them beyond railway company

police to check the empty cars
to ensure there is no such thing
as a free ride in this society
but they have music each other
energy of youth great hopes

I rest in this city comfort as
 fifty million birds hone their journey
overhead cutting through high cloud
heading on a course etched in molecules
magnetised in their wings
relentlessly driving them without doubt
 or fear to arctic nesting grounds

when I sleep my dreams have voices
Star and banjo sing her
song about the lost women on
the north's highway of tears
two longs, one short, one long whistle
her train approaches a level crossing
somewhere in stunted spruce country
in this house a baby cries soon soothed
 high in the tundra snow geese
light on the treeless land with life partners
nest in the slanted Arctic light
they have time only to feed the family

before their compass pulls them south
all passengers on an ever moving planet
they know home when they get there.

A beach in paradise

"I was put on this earth to change it." Kathe Kollwitz

palm fronds whisper to the cloudless sky
forever blue in the tropical sun
waves career joyfully over coral sands
every grain shifts with each wave
blinking and glistening like tiny mirrors
 postcard perfect for tourist brochures.

the beach is empty in the small bay
open to distant continents
curving into more palm trees
under the palms the intermittent
thud of dropping coconuts
light swallowed by the forest beyond.

a couple with a little girl arrives
strip down to bathing suits
the man stretches out and falls
asleep under his hat he dreams of
successful surgery and healthy babies
late nights in operating rooms.

the girl is engrossed by the pink sand
on the beach edge creates a temporary

topography of valleys and streambeds
watches the sea water enter and
retreat with hidden rhythms as it shifts
landscapes with every surge.

now the woman joins the inviting water
delighted by the comfort and silky feel
of the womb warm sea its power to
create movement with weightless ease
only waist high she splashes until she feels
her legs tugged out below her

she cannot gain foothold
she is pulled into deep water
her swim strokes useless, she shouts
at the child who screams as she runs
to waken the man they come running
down the beach desperate in their horror

from the darkness of tree trunks
comes a young man in shorts
he plunges in picks up the woman
under one arm and returns to the shore
he refuses all thanks and rewards
and disappears into the dense forest.

the family pack up, numb still with fear
and relief, leave the empty beach in paradise.

For thirty years now they ponder still
wondering about grace and meaning.

The security guard

A tall, sandy, young man
he loped over to us, friendly
like a golden retriever, came
to greet us at the slick chain hotel.
He knew we'd come for the hearing.
- *I'm security to keep the peace,*
not just for the judge, but you too,
 worked ten years
a policeman
on the streets of Vancouver.
I saw things I don't want
to remember.
I hate violence.
I hope this hearing will be peaceful -
he turned to leave
- *time to go in and get set up -*
 then
- *Don't tell them I said it*
but give them Hell,
I get the creeps just thinking
about those nukes out there.

We left the sun and walked
into our shadows
to assemble

in the gloom of judgment,
a dusty, sunless room,
the "hearing officer"
 a judge with a mind empty of metaphor
crammed with legal minutiae
his words were sharp silica,
erosion against our passion.
For him even our logic was
too remote, our love of light,
of life, irrelevant
to the legislation.
Assaulted by his letters
of the law, we spoke and left.
We breathed again
in the sun outside
said goodbye to
our peaceful guard

Indifferent to our haste,
he talked
- once
I knew a Japanese woman
in Vancouver,
she had really
unusual tattoos,
one day
I asked her about them -
His words blew past me

as I tried to get away
going home.
 then
- *she told me:*
these are
not tattoos
but
the pattern
of the
kimono
I was
wearing
the day
they
dropped
the bomb
on
Hiroshima.

A poem written after attending the Nanoose Bay, BC.
Expropriation hearing in 1999

August evening in Saskatchewan

For Louise

outside the city
to prairie hills
an orange sun climbed down
the western sky
as harvest moon rises in glorious
fullness in the east
beauty enough to fill our hearts
when my friend says come

we wander through Saskatoon bushes
goldenrod, sweet sage, thistles
young poplars birches with
leaves the size of thumb nails
happy in a trance of golden light
over a small hill we found a slough
in a broad valley with fading rushes and reeds
edged with prairie grasses

 we lie flat quiet and still
beside cracked boulders glowing with orange lichen
we splay ourselves on the shady slope
we cover patient waiting crocuses
over earth's heartbeat

we catch the sound mounting in waves
rolling rattles hoarse croaks
hosts of grey cloud reflect in the slough

hundreds of cranes descend
long legs skim our faces
they settle with clatter of consensus
wade content as they scoop
sharp bills through grasses
and life filled swamp water
one more night to fuel for
the return to a land without winter

we sink deeper in the land
knowing as they do to
stay means to become
frozen angels in the snow.

Refugia

Arctic outflow   enters the
chasm of   blankets between us
as you   move.
I pull you to   my valley
we intertwine
toes to toes
heels rubbing ankles
your tropical breath
falls through   my hair
until
my nape skin glows
hands hold fast
to other's familiar   mysteries
parts worn smooth   with
tides of touch
until we   twist in bundles
like a Mobius strip
endless   with only one surface.

We arrange in comfort
this refugia
from   a shifting landscape
where change   stalks
determined

to metamorphose
to disassemble
to transform.

The sound of silence

The sound of silence is an oyster, closed on a sandstone
outcrop waiting for the tide to return.

The sound of silence is the Queen of the Night opening
blossom at dusk, petals exhale the essence of jungle sex.

The sound of silence is in a star punctured Arctic sky
as Aurora unfolds undulating curtains of light.

The sound of silence is my pillow waiting
for the Pleiades shower on a warm summer night.

The sound of silence is in the earth, a myriad
of creatures eating their way through soil, making soil.

Precious in their commonness: herring gulls, mallard
ducks, pelagic cormorants, everyday murders of crows.

When they are gone we shall hear
the sound of silence forever.

Birch bark love letter

She pulled back her long dark hair
and formed a knot
that stretched her eyes into shadowy canyons
trapped by the wooden clasp, he had carved
on a better brighter day than this
evening of earth-toned sky
already fermenting and decaying toward darkness.

She walked away from prying eyes
along the riverbank where she had so carefully
in noon's innocent expectance
washed her skin and tossed her hair
at the other women's teasing.

Now she slipped through the pines
her shadow one with theirs
weaving like boughs in the strengthening gusts
while she composed her words;
but first to a spinney of birth
stems still holding light,
tattered with last season's curled news.

Her knife was sharp steel
traded from the Urals
for many furs that mother scraped and cleaned

so daughter too could call her life
woman, basket-maker, woodcutter,
skinner, sewer, harvester.

She peeled the scroll
of clearest bark parchment
enough for the plainest of eternal messages.
She held it flat with stones
on glacier scrubbed granite
not aware her knees called in pain
against the crystalline hardness
as she pulled her knife through every word.

There high above the settlement
she could watch a door closed
like eyelids of the dead.
No sound but the pain of
her engraving on living tree flesh
echoed by the taunt of crows
disturbed in their message making.
Where were you last night?
Why didn't you come?
Don't you love me anymore?
enough, but not ready yet, she adds,
I waited for you by the moss bank long past sundown.

Then she sheathed her blade
in the river roar her hair clasp

made no splash or ripple
when it entered the frothy rapids.
she yanked long strands from her scalp
then bound them round the scroll
and watched the moon rise half empty.
Next day he found the roll and tossed it unread
in another damp moss bank
laughing when he heard the cooing calls
rising and falling through the glade.

*CBC news item: "The oldest birch bark love letter ever
found was discovered recently in Siberia. Experts date the
missive at over 1000 years old."*

Shell, sea and skin

my shell is weeping through parchment
translucent skin so sheer
that my veins protrude reveal my
shameless passion broadcast my fears

skin so vulnerable and public
wars and lovers engrave
their histories in blood and steel
beyond boundaries and barricades

I never cease my constant motion
always unprotected that sunlight may
blind my eyes and erase wounding
memory of struggle to enclose beauty

membranes can barely hold back
the waters of my body's sea
to contain this my blood or
stay the spilling into oceanic oblivion

hidden in the tidal zone you remain discreet
the whole world can see the moon
hanging open to bewitch beholders
 you conceal another moon within your shell

amniotic tides wash you on your journey
to becoming a fossil with the tenacity of peace
you transform sand to pearl create a moon
that decrees your fate to die for beauty.

Sandals

summer vibrates from the pavement
Beirut shimmers in the fierce sun
two friends meet happily
complain about the heat
look forward to school starting soon
one has sore feet heat swollen
her shoes are too tight
so they exchange shoes
laughing as they hop around and
support each other while
indulgent adults smile at their antics
one goes home nearby in the tight shoes
the other now comfortable in white sandals
sun twinkling on brass buckles
dances off to meet her favourite
uncle for a drive into the country.

later after the explosion
investigators find in the car rubble
legs severed at the knee
on the feet clean white sandals
buckles still gleaming in the light.

Ghassian Kanafani and his niece, Lamis, were killed in a car bomb, July 8, 1972 in Beirut. The poem is dedicated to my friend, Sima, who lives in Amman. She is the friend in the poem who lent Lamis her sandals.

Bread

they lie in rows
plump and sweet
like freshly washed
baby bottoms
I bend down and
tenderly caress a cheek
with powdery softness
it sighs and gently subsides
cover them with cloth
to puff again
I leave them warm in
their growing mystery
strong wheat
from Saskatchewan's plain
shapes and holds the air
traps the promise
of ancient Sumeria

soon the food of Gods
will present itself
enclosing
the bones of
Riel and Dumont
their bread was
hastily baked

beside a wagon
on their flight
from men's eternal folly.

somewhere near Babylon
another woman kneads
her meagre ration
not knowing if it is the last
weary from worry
unable to flee the madness
rampant in ancient empires.

we can only bless the steaming
loaves and rejoice
in the renewal of life.

Porphyry

Imbedded in a matrix
indistinguishable and uniform
forged by
fiery upheaval
clear crystals appear
grow like snowflakes
in the wintry sky
each unique
to create a stone of strength
that itself
crumbles in history
to sand
of dynasties
now obliterated
souls conspire
pass their radiant messages
to events yet unshaped.

The journalist's war

the soldier lies on the stony ground
his machine on a tripod
encircled by a bandolier of bullets
each a separate glistening jewel
each a shining death.
his cherubic face, flushed
looks up at her, a sweet child adult.
she did not know he still carried
wax crayons and a colouring book of animals
to remember the family farm

the journalist has been to more wars
than he has ever known
she is bitter cynical
actually she hates soldiers
most of them are life's losers
can't make it in the real world
like this kid, she bets he can barely read
that night he stepped on a roadside bomb
she takes a photo of
his entrails-splattered remains
sees glints of primary colours

she walks away and gets his name
files her story keeps the photo one day
she'll blow it up and see the broken stubs
of wax crayons gleaming in his bleeding flesh.

To the girl in the bikini

with butterscotch skin and honey hair
in the innocent confidence
of youth you stroll by
licking an ice cream cone
your body smooth and unsullied
as sweet confection
your pleasure an act of communion
you saunter beside funky shops
sheltered by tall firs
signalled by circling golden eagles
when you walk
the atoll of your breasts seal-slick
shimmers above your careful tan
your bikini acknowledges no tragedy
sightless beauty does not understand
the horror of decades past
crimes of present times
you are too young for history
we are Women in Black
a group in silence
you do not notice us shaded by
a red Japanese cherry
 mourning nuclear destruction
we ponder intelligence in denial

we think of another island
on the dark side of the earth
while we stand in noon's sun
an island where there are
no cows for cream
no gardens for fat melons
where palms drop mutant fruit
food comes on supply ships
when toxic soil cannot nurture life
I see on the palette of your glowing skin
the poison plumes begin to develop
shadows and fissures emerge   your skin sears
you become a map of the Bikini Atoll
two bombs on cities and twenty-two
nuclear bomb tests later.

Low tide

meadows of sea lettuce exposed
 by afternoon's low tide
stretch across the bay
as the sum turns north
I pick my way through
the slippery forage
avoid purple sea stars
they want to stay wet during
their wait for tide's turn
gulls at the water's edge
are importantly busy
the politicians of the beach
opportunistically meet and eat
the compliant whelks
eagles fly over
looking for easy kills
then perch together
start a soprano duet
their range far more suitable
for a seed eating thrush
 their trill a brilliant disguise
for a greedy scavenger hunt
I greet the only other visitor
we go our separate ways
the beach is vast

and respects solitudes
under the treed banks
I look for eagle feathers
yet knowing
they won't be found by looking

I find a maybe
 maybe eagle
 maybe gull
maybe goose
the sea has worked it too hard
I reject its skeletal remains
sit on a log to think about
a story I am writing
about a friend across this water
across the world
some molecules of this cold sea
may turn warm as they lap her shoreline
distracted by a piece of drifted cedar
the knots and twisted grain
shape a monkey face
I feed it liquorice all-sorts
of fine banded pebbles
and round granites covered
with nonpareils of barnacle feet
until land lines pull me back
to tasks uncompleted
my words are winnowed by

dense brambles that invade the trail
where spring roses
scatter by thousands
petals of memory
I leave the sea to its work
I am called to mine.

Bones are cast

An erratic arc
threatens prophecy
as the clatter shudders into silence
woven into a pattern
with hidden intention
bones cover chaos
reveal our frailty
remind us
of our destiny as
no prophecy can
life ends
life continues.

The leg

I saw it on a side street in Arles
shady and deserted
away from the proud Roman arena
and rows of tourist shops empty
during the slow French lunch break
in a dusty shop window
full of unwanted junk

It gleamed in its past
glory of flaunted service
showing off those precious
fifteen denier hose
we rolled up so carefully
to prevent dreaded runs
 to ensure seams straight.

A Lucite leg, perfect
from its pointed toes and classic arch
to sinuously curved calf
and gently opening thigh
the thick bit above the stocking top
like my leg thirty years ago
both now serve less glamorous purposes.

I saw you there, enclosed within

gleaming orange, swishing
your tiny frilled fins and plump fretwork body
as you gulped along the surface of that
full still promise.

I circled demurely from heel to knee
sending messages of adoration
in tiny perfect bubbles until
bored with your preoccupation
I flashed golden and bold
through the shaft of light
of one feeble lamp in that dark display
my frail translucent fins and tail
determined in their upward strokes.

I joined you on the edge of freedom
in the flute of our transparent captivity,
together we sipped gleefully
our champagne of numinous delight.

Uganda night

We are both still
under our own
mosquito nets
not wanting to sleep yet
bats squeal
radar soundings
against dense branches
insects call with sounds
of scratched legs
the murmur of Luo
of the workers meeting
in the relief of darkness
fractures our words, our thoughts
into the text of displacement,
only senses, sensations, sensuousness
have meaning, the clove scent of
skin raises cilia
to attend, then taste
the thickened night
until axes falter
lands drift plates shift
our hands touch through the strata
traverse eons, eras, epochs
when we tended together
the spice plants of the same sun

the skin of our geology

our species saturated with shared history
we join under our separate canopies
of present division.

No Tenemos Que Pedir Permiso Para Ser Libres*

Well-fed tourists, hungry for exotica
gawk at the sunlit façade an old Spanish cathedral
in older Mesozoic mountains where doves moan on
precipices on angels freshly painted mustard amarillo.

Brown shadows scuttle on
sharp edges of history under walls
of Maya and Moors symbols of power long gone
Christ still bleeds on the cross inside
these walls well impregnated with male urine.

Centuries pass they come and come
conquistadores all white and strong
blind in armour of self-belief
construct of global power.

A big man a pale foreigner his thick slugs of arms
swoops upon a scrap of humanity
filthy in a black skirt the rest mud coloured
her legs frail twigs of earth.

Her terror ignored he laughs guffaws of glee
My God! he laughs where is glee in this girl child?

maybe five years old who falls
in rigid fear from his fleshy noose

She vanishes from the worn pavement
into cracks of lost time to die within a year.

*We Do Not Have To Ask Permission In Order To Be Free.
(Zapatista slogan on grandstand in front of cathedral,
San Cristobal de las Casas, Mexico)

Chiapas: Plenary

A bunched plenary of clouds
huddles over San Cristobal
agrees to strike on dusty streets below
where on flood-safe raised stone ways
God's creatures danced their destinies
for five centuries on even
more ancient pathways.

Two women, Mayan in their compact darkness,
probably sisters, moving in chiaroscuro
one wears a red huipil
a threaded mythology across her breasts
crimson ribbons interwoven in her braid
that curves like a mountain range
to merge in the earth of black wool skirt
her thickened feet fit
in smooth stone caressed by her foremother's heel.

the other in skirt of cheap floral print
of everywhere's global factory
wears a faded pink T-shirt
exhorting winning power to
Washington Redskins
her neon green sandals slip
as first drops strike.

Joining hands the sisters run
past a cardboard sign hand lettered
"your name on a grain of rice"
into the supermercado,
juntas, together; *siempre,* forever.

Asleep in La Selva

clouds in floating scarves
        catch on the next valley
citrus-hued finches and tanagers
    perch silent
in the high canopy
even vultures cease to swirl
above
      army's stolen slaughter
every
     bone
        scrape
            of hide
shredded flesh: engorged.

the surviving cattle stream
      in silver
   humps swaying
        like lost continents
on seas of algae
        lowing into port.
as white egrets
fold sails
in lambent
      mahogany masts.

the Lacandon hills
    iridescent   like grackles' wings
sucking the final
                crepuscular light
until crusts of stars are strewn
             like lost souls
    crying inside   crickets.

waiting dogs get their chance
to yelp detection
at prowling soldiers
Tzeltals sleep
in their hammocks
     slung
like fingers
on the earth's pulse.

when dogs sleep
       and crickets' legs sing
Tzeltals dream
       of mariposa wings
transformed
   into cloaks of liberty
       and flowers in La Selva
exhale elusive
       perfumes of peace.

and one lone piper
        eases the night
with reedy pavans
          calling
             calling
                calling
to the forgetful ancestors.

In Kudankalum under the banyan tree: *Aswath Vriksha*

"I am Banyan, tree among trees" · *Bhagavad Gita*

*A poem for the women of Kudankalum village
and in memory of Rosalie Bertell*

Eyes of the world
briefly flutter on this village
a patch of baked mud
around a solitary Banyan tree
this earth has bloomed in swaying blossoms
hundreds of women
 saris wrapped around their heads their bodies
 fragile shields against sun's heat
 woven in every conceivable tint and hue
of nature's generous world
 they sit and plan determined
to save their seeds
cloistered in wombs wrapped in silk and cotton
no protection from radiation.

they may not know how to write
or to read any human constructed language
but they understand messages from their bodies

like divine *Ashwath Vriksha*
they carry seeds of eternal life
unto countless generations
hidden in frail shell of their flesh
they can read messages of the atom from
Hiroshima to Fukushima
they prepare to starve to save the future
to save seeds of life from mutation
to protect their eggs that carry promise
of life for every succeeding generation
they sit and fast in sun's golden heat
try to imagine the white heat of explosions
 power of atoms divided
dust of deadly fallout.

 their message is simple
 no nuclear plants
 go to the sea for power
 reach to the sky for power
 let us live, fish, garden
in our earthly paradise
 leave the future to bloom in vivid colours
 let our granddaughters
 their granddaughters
dance a tapestry of swaying flowers
 with sacred banyan
Ashwath Vriksha for life eternal.

In San Isidro

Eugenia stands her legs braced
drawing force from the earth
energy moving up to her fists
clasped behind her apron
strong from the resistance of bread dough
her resistance to the injustice
of death by poison of gold mining
shaped in a loaf of bread
her horno for baking in a shaded garden
lush with fruit, vines, trees, beans for family
strength and pan dulse to sweeten her town
behind a high wall with a mural that tells
the world 'our resources are not merchandise'
we are life, trees, pure flowing water and bread
'resistance for life' is our daily meal.

Eugenia embraces life
with the joy of flying birds
even as a bullet with her name awaits
a phone call from Vancouver.

*Eugenia is an anti-mining activist in a community where
four other activists have been assassinated.*

The poet in the post office

for Carole Chambers, 1944 – 2014
Hornby Island. V0R1Z0

she weighs in grams the records
of this small community
exchanges smiles for stamps
fills up slots with the weight of
worries and limbs of trees
heavy words commanding control
bills, receipts, orders
in two official languages
urgent cries, love-filled sighs
and complaints
in many more

lines of poems unwritten
stick in the drawers
phrases tangle in piles of newspapers
words here can fly
or fizzle discarded or unnoticed
dreams are misplaced by
others' urgent needs
fragile webs of creation
cosset her imagination as
she tapes a parcel

registers a bill payment
sympathises with everyone's troubles

in the florescent fug of her domain
her legs ache
standing all day she adds up
the queen's coin
counts new stamps in endless sheets
dispatches concealed messages
of hope and sorrow
views her landscape
of cash machines,
magazine racks
drink coolers in the general store.

her head aches from the latest directives
of the distant corporation
intended to confound
bureaucrats in sterile offices
envy her forest and sea
they demand more counting,
recounting   accounting
until she and other fretted workers
howl in frustration laugh in rebellion
turn out the lights and they leave the documents
and numbers to dance with each other

she cycles cloaked in green drizzle

gripping her rough driveway as
cedars bend to guide her home
where she lies to rest beside her lover
her mouth on his ear
she can hear the bees feasting
on quince blossoms
behind her eyelids barred owls
glide silently through
drop talons of new words
for her to sort
to make into something as true
as beautiful as this moment.

Lightning Source UK Ltd.
Milton Keynes UK
UKHW011112151219
355424UK00006B/219/P